Copyright © 2022 by Daisy Ozim/Professional High Priestess

All rights reserved.

This book or any portion there of may not be reproduced or used in any manner what so ever without the express written permission of the publish except for the use of brief quotations in a book review.

Printed in the United States of America

First Printing, 2022
979-8-9864851-3-3
979-8-9864851-4-0

www.DaisyOzim.Co

HISTORY OF REIKI

Reiki which is actually known as the Zrakranrari is an ancient system of energy work created by the high priest and high priestess of energy warfare. Their names are Irnunuzwangwun and Irnwuzwugwanzwu. They crafted this system as a response to the high levels of energy harvesting and energetic attack they received due to their bloodline, spiritual abilities and the gifts, elements and resources located on their planet. The system of reiki we are currently accessing was created as a way to mimic their work in efforts to usurp them by a federation of banished peoples called the Grizirinsri which in ancient Japanese language means "the people with no source or connection to God". This is the translation in modern Japanese:

"がぎにゐせき"

They were banished, meaning the God code in their DNA was removed and destroyed due to their involvement in sexual deviancy, enslaving others and tampering with the works of several federations.

The existing system of reiki is filled with demonic, satanic and soul fracturing symbols that were given to a few individuals of this federation who then spread them amongst planet earth. They turned Reiki into a racket for westerners and racists who sought to make money off of the spiritual community.

For those who have been practicing Reiki, do not be alarmed. The high priest and high priestess have a specific system wherein, if you are not a karmic, they download the energy from the true symbols in your transmissions for you.

Those of you who are not allowed into this system because you're a racist, clout chasing or unbeknownst to you, your federation and or bloodline has been banished, you have not been accessing the Zkrakanrari. You have been downloading alien/demonic coding into your DNA and that of unsuspecting individuals who are just seeking healing. This is where your work comes in regarding denouncing the false system and carrying out the new one accurately with respect to those who created it.

ARGRANAZWANI
(In respects to God and the God in you)

SYMBOL TRANSLATIONS

The Following are the translations of the existing reiki symbols from the Usui and Karuna systems as well as the Zrakranrari equivalents

USUI/ KARUNA SYMBOL	ACTUAL MEANING	ZRAKRANRARI VERSION
	There will be a constant attack to your eternal existence by fracturing your Ingrairizwainai	ZRIRRAGRAWANZWAI
	The energy lacks a powerful force to carry it all the way through to manifestation	AGRAZWANADWANZA
	The demon of Gruawai (the strongest sex demon) will descend upon you and siphon your spiritual force indefinitely	NO EQUIVALENT
	The energy will never conduct in a consistent manner	GRIGRAWANI
	There are opposing forces which will create constant disharmony	GRAIZWAINWAIKRANKRAI

USUI/ KARUNA SYMBOL	ACTUAL MEANING	ZRAKRANRARI VERSION
	I will create a loop hole in your energy to keep siphoning your life force	ZAGRAWANAU
	I will loosen up your energy systems to enter into your space and drain you with the Grizriwainai	ZRINIGRAIWATRAYA
	A force will descend upon you and unravel your Zraigraiwanai (the spiral of eternal life and force)	ZAKRAI ZWANKANAZWI
	A force will capture your strongest essence and route it to the three pronged demon of lust, greed and desire	BRAIWAINWAIZWAI
	A force will split yourZraigraiwanai	GRUZWUNAIZWAI
	THe force that separates the water element of intuition from the fire element of the spirit mind	ZRIGRIWINTRIRSRI

USUI/ KARUNA SYMBOL	ACTUAL MEANING	ZRAKRANRARI VERSION
	You will bring no energy towards you	NO EQUIVALENT
	A barrier will be placed between you and your Zaygrazininwa (the highest intuitive force)	ZRIKRIRINRINRI
	A force descends upon you to invert your energetic functions and route your proper force to the Irgrauwuzai	ZWIRNWIRTRANCRA
	The life force will be unraveled, drained and lack a conductive force	ZANGRANWINI
	A cube with portals on all sides will be placed over you allowing the AYGRIZINZI (the demon of energetic vampirism) to come over all of your forms.	NO EQUIVALENT
	The pineal gland will have no access to its natural state of function	NO EQUIVALENT

USUI/ KARUNA SYMBOL	ACTUAL MEANING	ZRAKRANRARI VERSION
	"The soul will be fractured in two with no ability to be unified to the original source.	BRAIWANZAIWANZINAI
	A force will constantly create a fragmentation to the Zrintringzrao (the master energ body)	IRZRIGRARANDRANDRIRNRA
	I call on the demon of Grandazwanai to create a complete blockage between you and your higher selves.	NO EQUIVALENT
	There is no meaning here. Only a portal of confusion that will open upon use	NO EQUIVALENT

BASICS OF ZRAKRANRARI

This system functions off of the archetype of 8 which correlates to the universal force that is present in all things that are of the highest source which is God. You will always invoke the 8 when using any of the symbols used in this system.

 ARGRAIZAWANI: The master spiral which aligns with the highest source of energy. Always with 8 rings

 GRANWAI: Representing a reduction in a negative force

 IRGUNZWAI: Representing a complete blockage in a force

 AGUAZENWA: The element of water

 ZAGWANAIZWAI: The element of air

 ZIGRITRIZWI: The element of fire

 AGRIDWENWAI: The element of earth

HOW TO USE THIS SYSTEM

This is a simple system that only requires you stay in alignment with what is true. When you choose to go back and forth between stable behavior and karmic behavior, it will not work for you. For those who have engaged in the prior reiki system, you can first clear yourself of the karmic/alien frequencies and then align yourself with this system through the attunement process.

STEP 1: MASTER CLEARING

The first step is completely clearing the soul of false soul ties, alien frequencies and karmic energies in order for the next steps to have a stronger effect and gain the most from your use of this system. You will invoke the GRAGRAZANRI by drawing it on your photo and putting it to fire or meditating on the symbol.

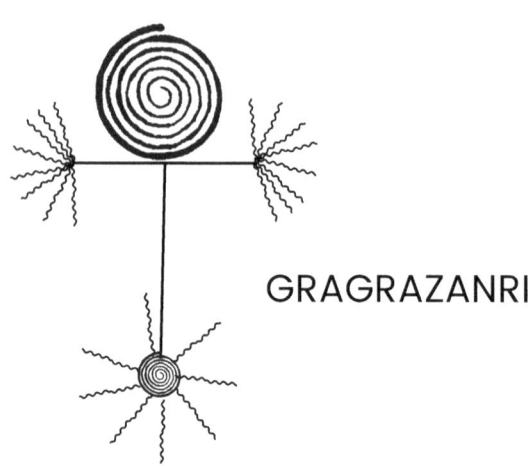

GRAGRAZANRI

STEP 2: MASTER REALIGNMENT

After clearing the soul on all levels, you invoke the ARZRANAGRANSRINRI to connect to God on all levels. This will alter your enter existence and align you with the highest universal force of energy which is karma free, without the guru effect and supports your higher selves as well.

ARZRANAGRANSRINRI

STEP 3: MASTER ATTUNEMENT

After clearing the soul and re-establishing or enforcing the connection to God aka the universal life force, you will then invoke the AGRAGRAZWANDWANZA which aligns you with all of your higher selves. This is important because DNA upgrades, downloads and gifts come from our higher selves. In order to move forward spiritually, you must be in alignment with your higher selves. This will lead to a more fulfilling spiritual life which automatically invokes more protection and awareness as a byproduct,

AGRAGRAZWANDWANZA

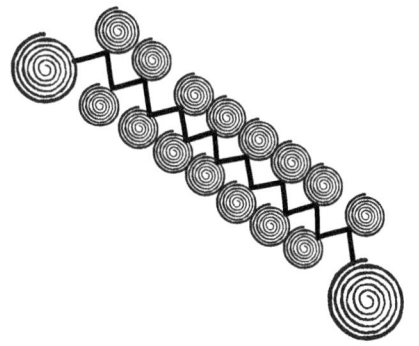

AFTER CLEARING, ATTUNEMENT & REALIGNMENT

After engaging in the aforementioned process to realign yourself with the universal force, you should undertake the following activities.

HYDRATE

Drink plenty of water before and after. This helps to institute the rapid change of cells and DNA in the body to allow for an entire transformation of the physical body, the ESP system and the nervous system which are all interconnected and manage the intuition and what we know as downloads which is an internal system for information processing

REST/MEDITATE

You will receive a boost in energy and a redesign to your energetic systems which will alter your processes within the body, mind and ether (astral body, synonymous bodies). It's important to rest afterwards and meditate to integrate the change. Like detoxing, a stripping of old energies will allow you to better embrace the new.

GROUND & REFLECT

Grounding the body with supplements such as magnesium and carbon allow the transmission to take hold within the energy field as these two elements are a base for the substance that comprises the energy field. Taking notes on the downloads you receive will help as well.

ZRAKRANRI SYMBOLS

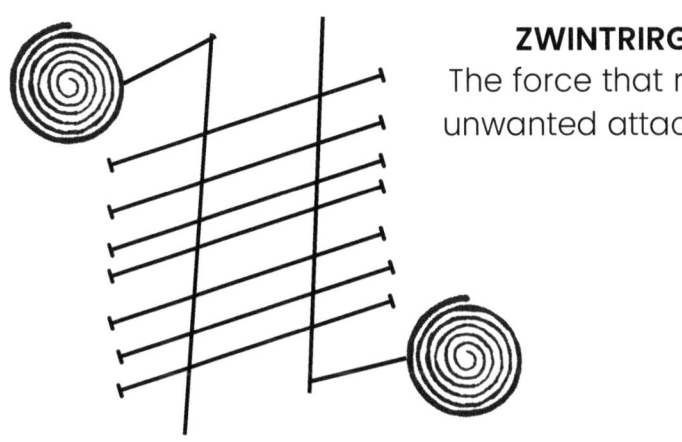

ZWINTRIRGRIR
The force that removes unwanted attachments.

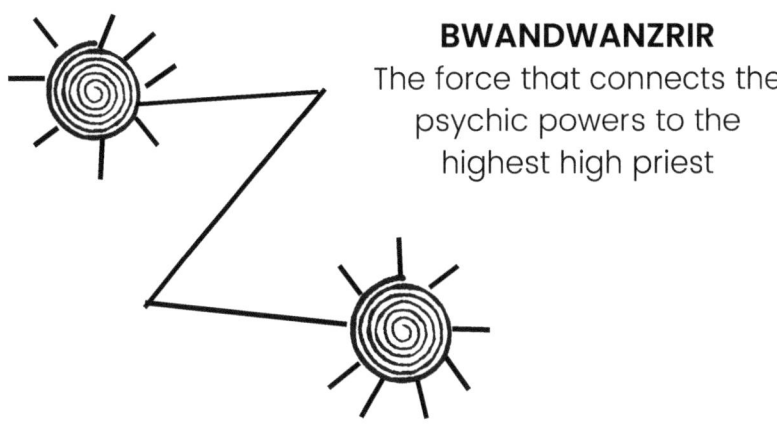

BWANDWANZRIR
The force that connects the psychic powers to the highest high priest

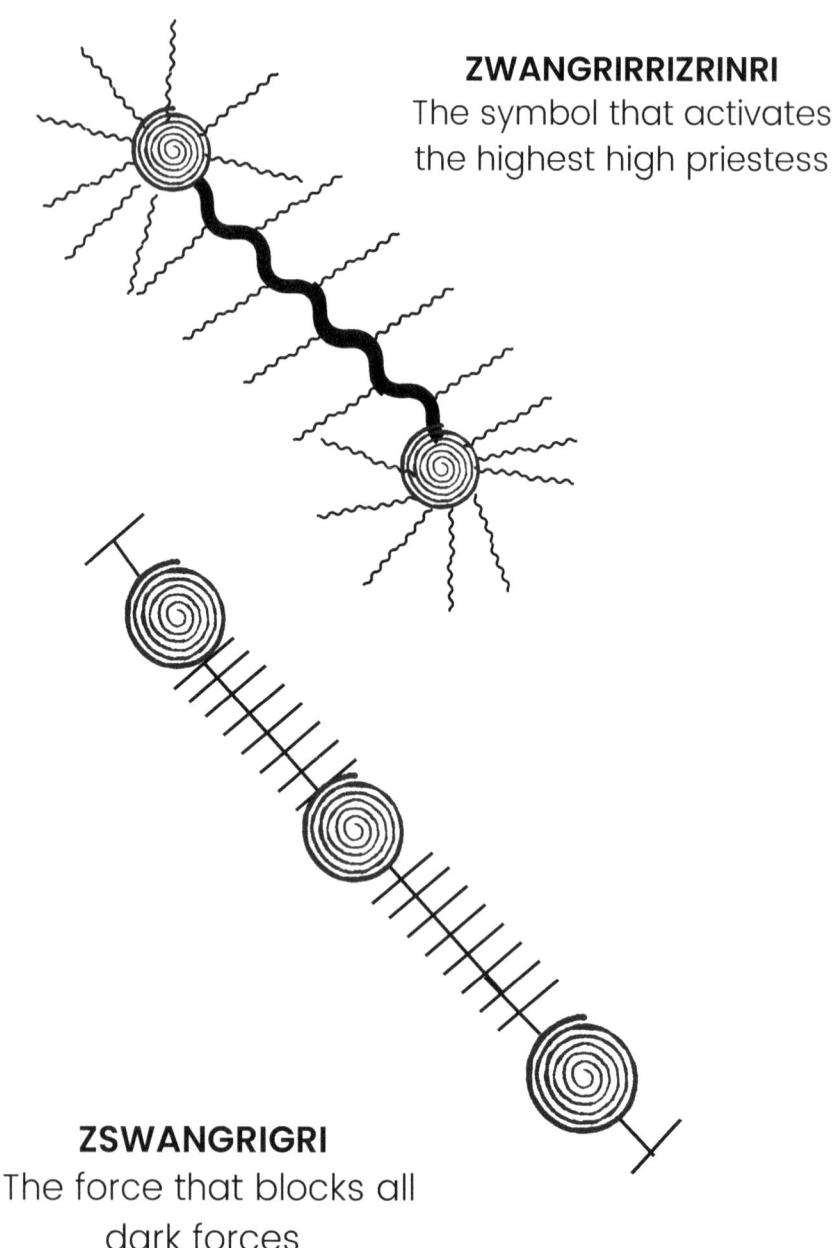

ZWANGRIRRIZRINRI
The symbol that activates the highest high priestess

ZSWANGRIGRI
The force that blocks all dark forces

GIRGRAGWINI
The force that unravels darkness from the soul

BRIRBRACKRADANWANI
The force that brings complete destruction to the enemy

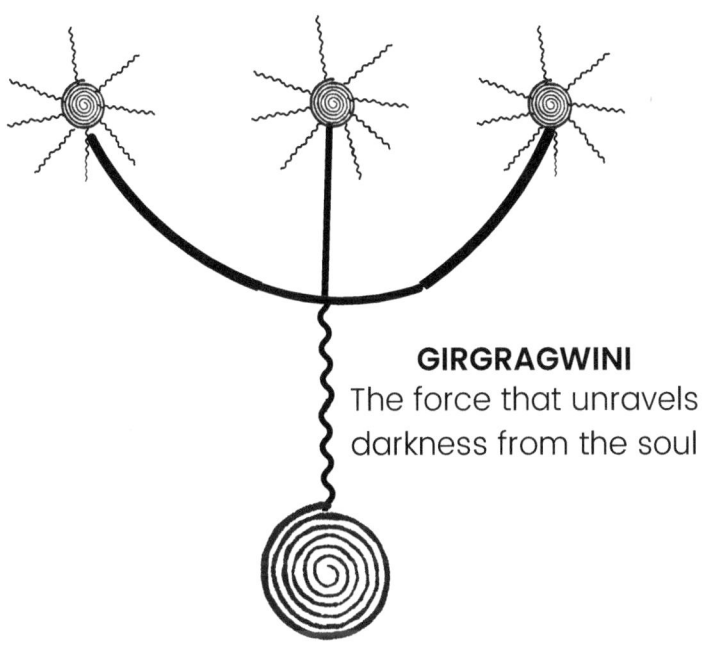

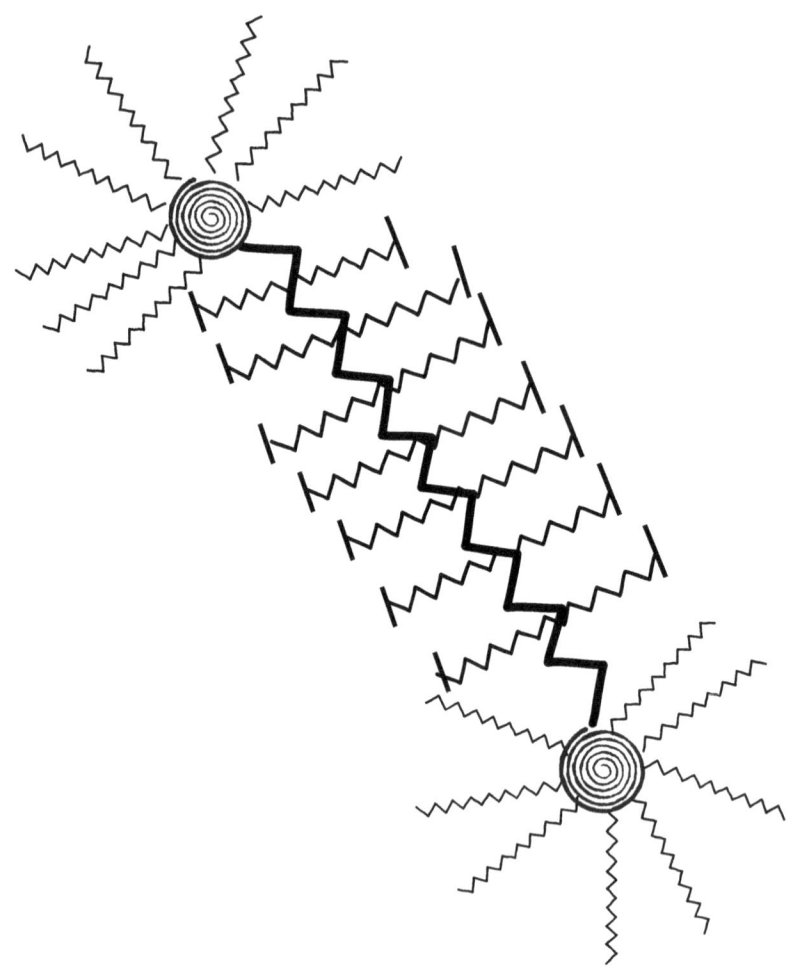

BRAGRAGWANDARI
The force that blocks any and all attacks.

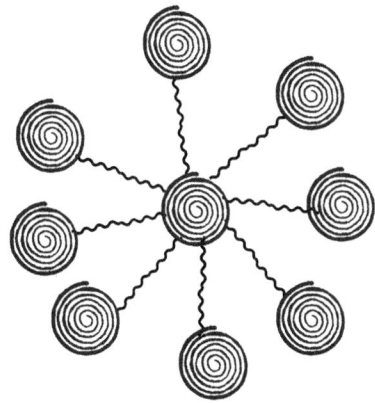

BAGRAGWADARI
The force that heals the effects of trauma on the soul

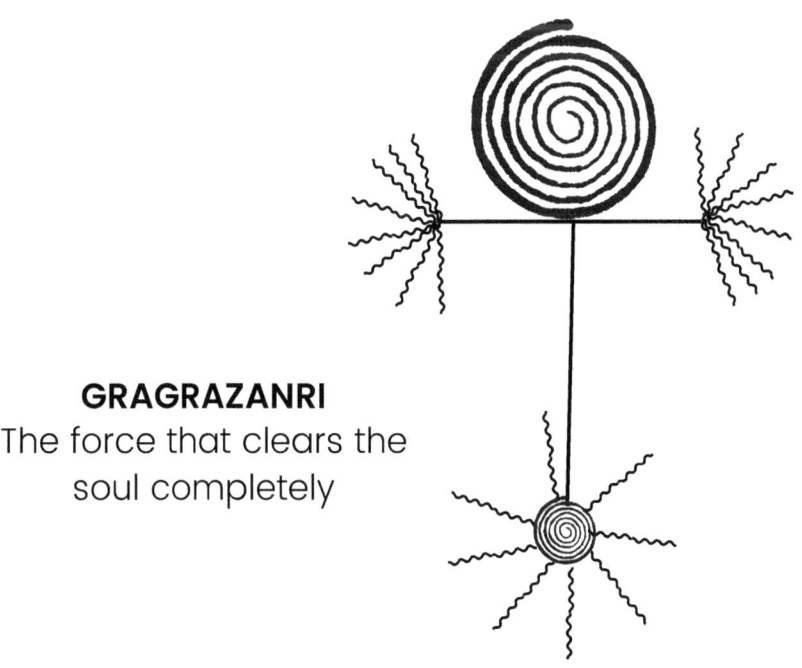

GRAGRAZANRI
The force that clears the soul completely

ZWINBRAGRAWANDAWI
The force that brings chaos to evil doers.

ZRINGRANGRARANTRANCRA
The force that heals the DNA

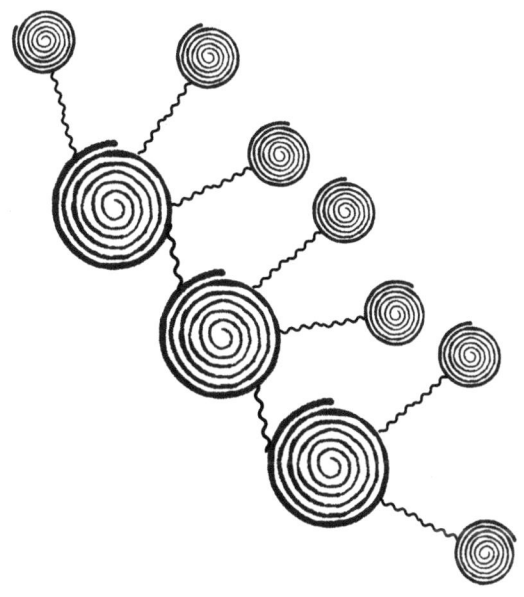

GRAGRAWAINDAI
The work that rectifies the soul on all levels

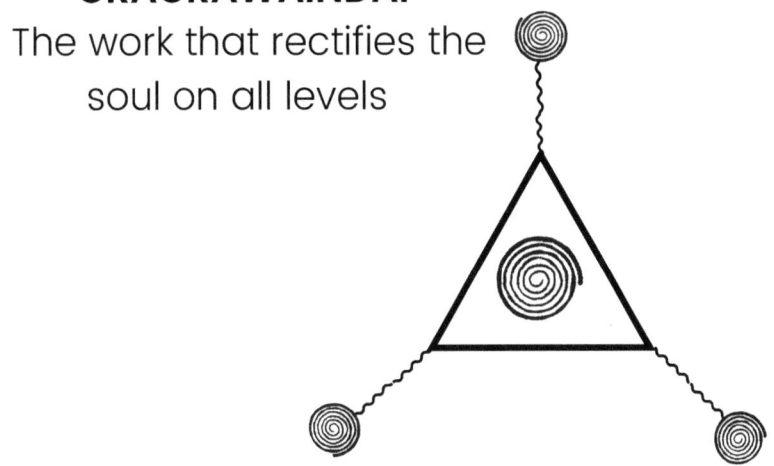

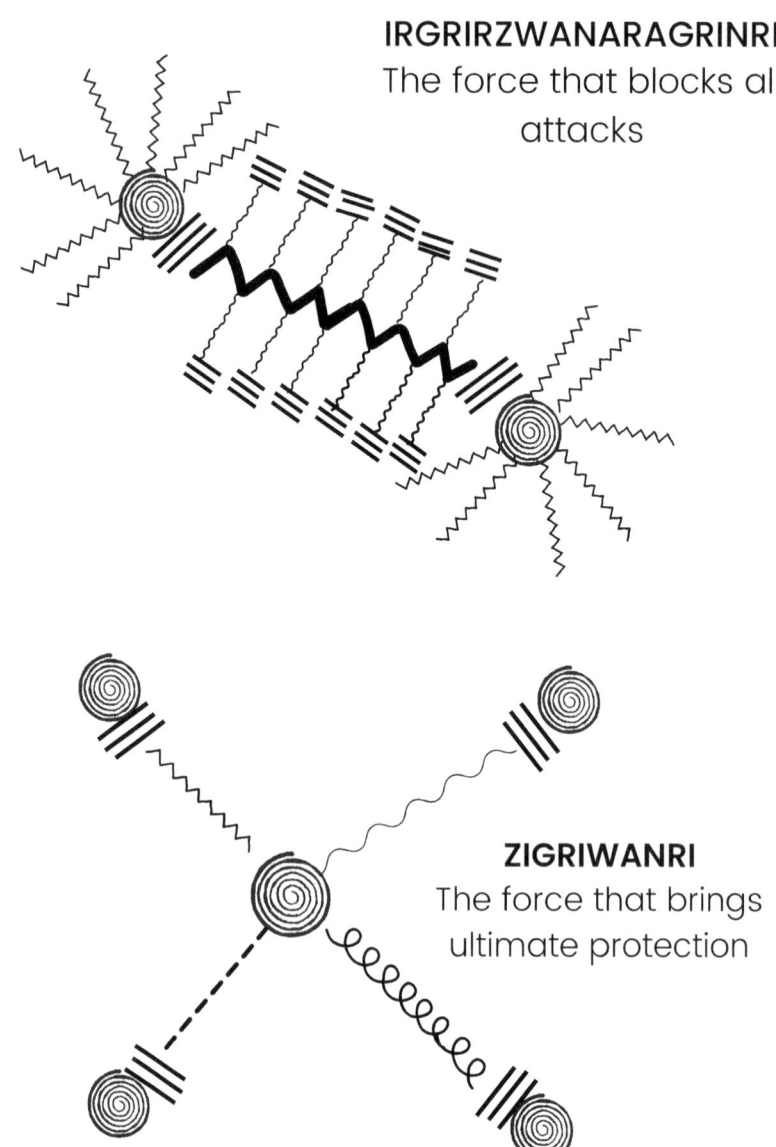

IRGRIRZWANARAGRINRI
The force that blocks all attacks

ZIGRIWANRI
The force that brings ultimate protection

ZWANGRANGRIRZRIRRI
The force that renews and stabilizes the physical body

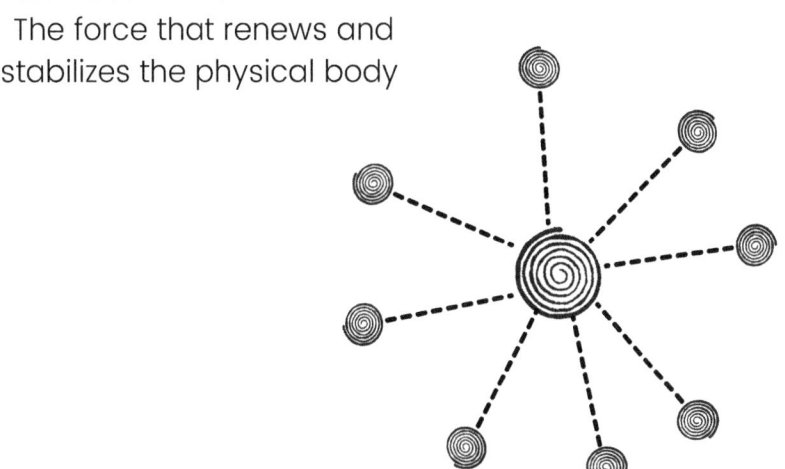

ARZRANAGRANSRINRI
The force that invokes and reestablishes the connection to God

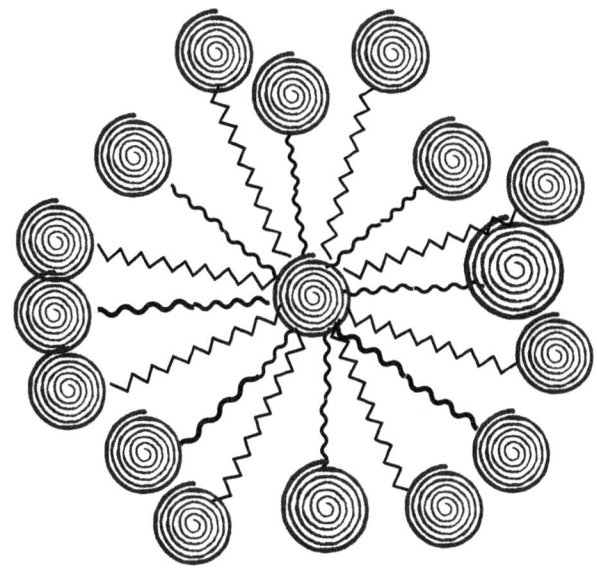

ZAGRANWANCRANCRI
The force that stabilizes the fire of the spirit

BRIZRINRIRNI
The force that destroys negativity on all levels of the spirit

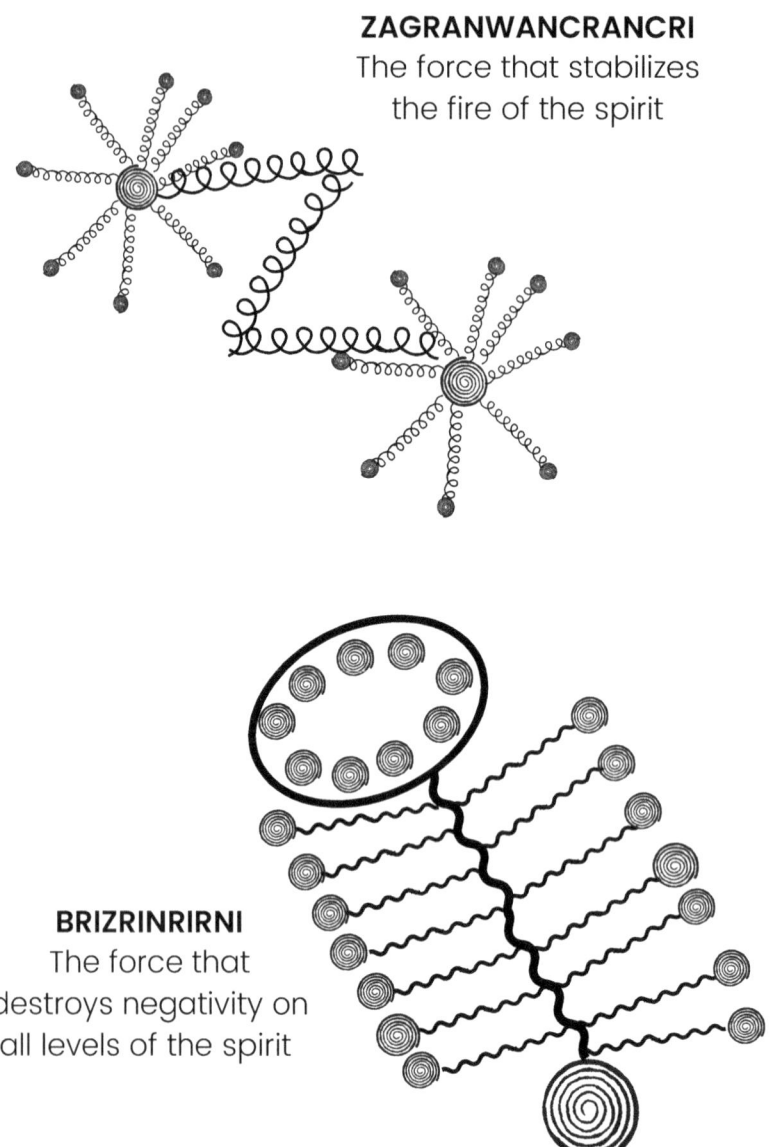

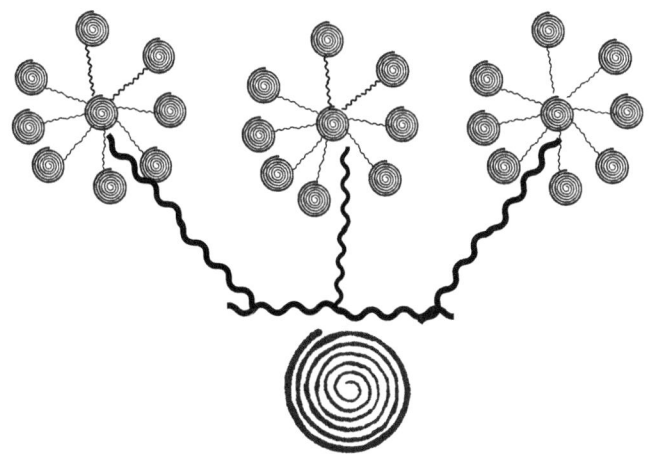

DWANWANAGRANGRIRZRIR
The force that destroys enemies
of God between lovers

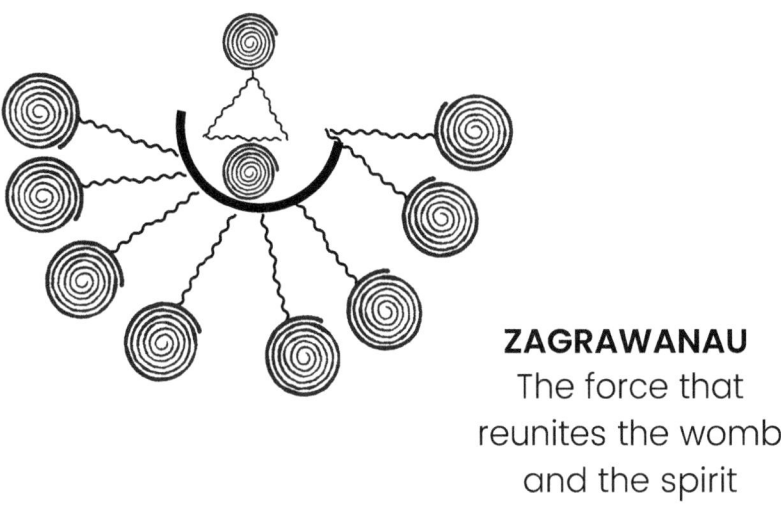

ZAGRAWANAU
The force that
reunites the womb
and the spirit

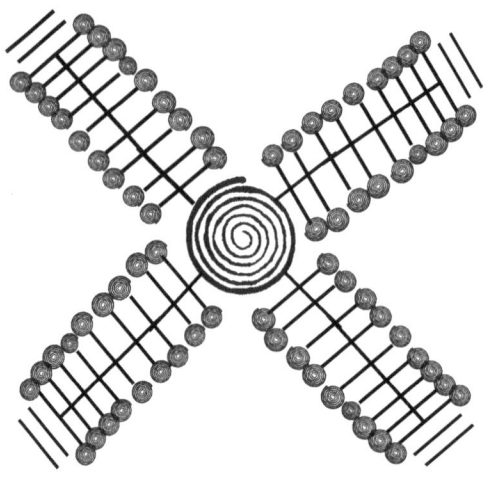

ARGRAGRAWANE
The force that eliminates all fallacies from the soul and higher bodies.

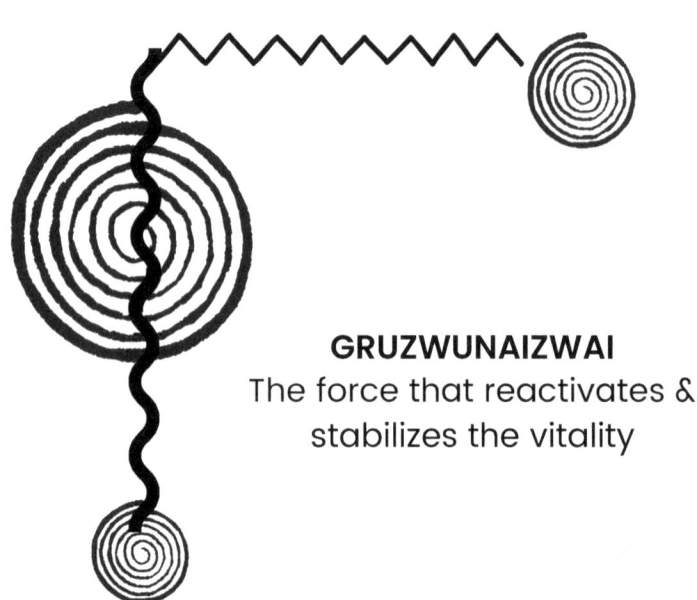

GRUZWUNAIZWAI
The force that reactivates & stabilizes the vitality

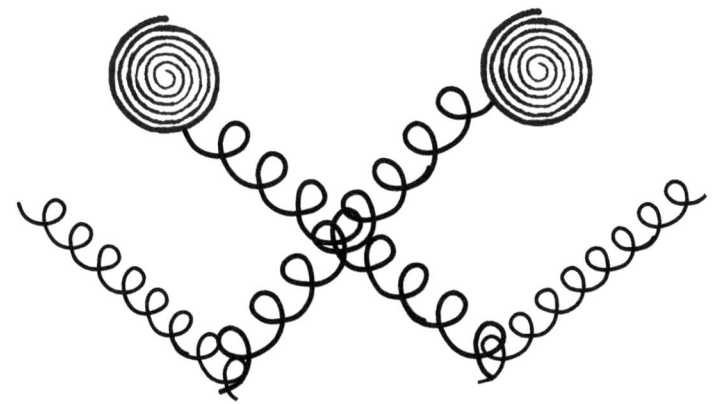

ZRIKIRIZRINI
The force that eliminates all fallacies from the soul and higher bodies.

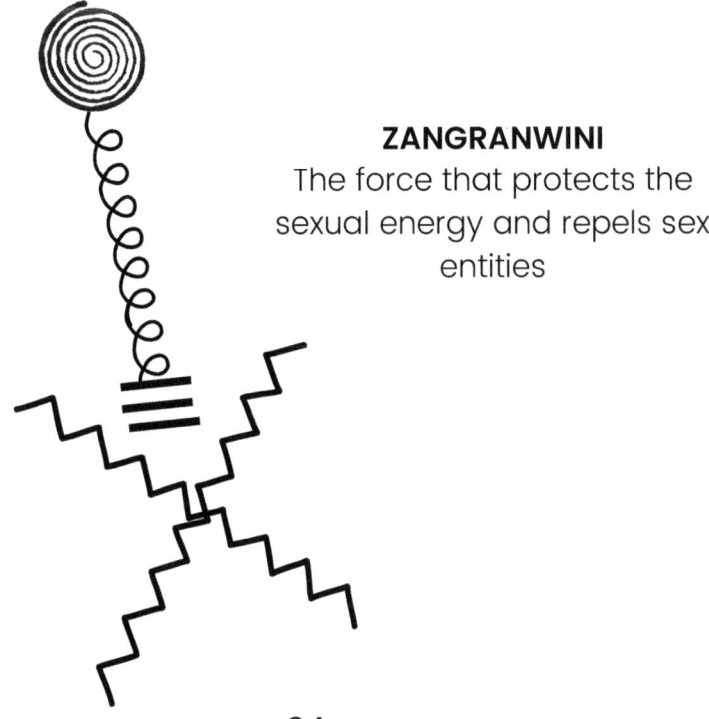

ZANGRANWINI
The force that protects the sexual energy and repels sex entities

ZRIGRIWINTRIRSRI
The force that reunifies the mind & the soul

ZWIRNWIRTRANCRA
The force that reunites mind, body & soul to work in unison

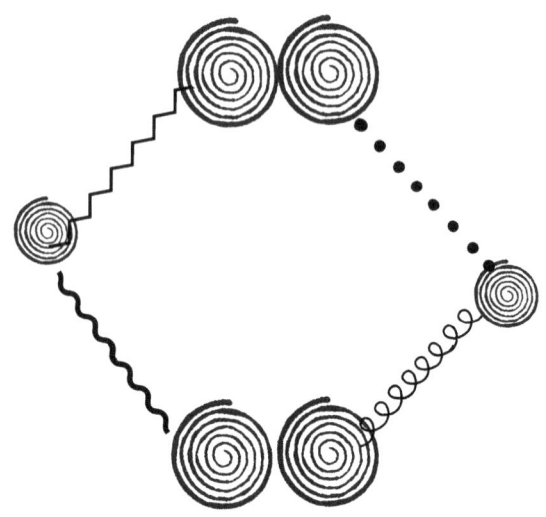

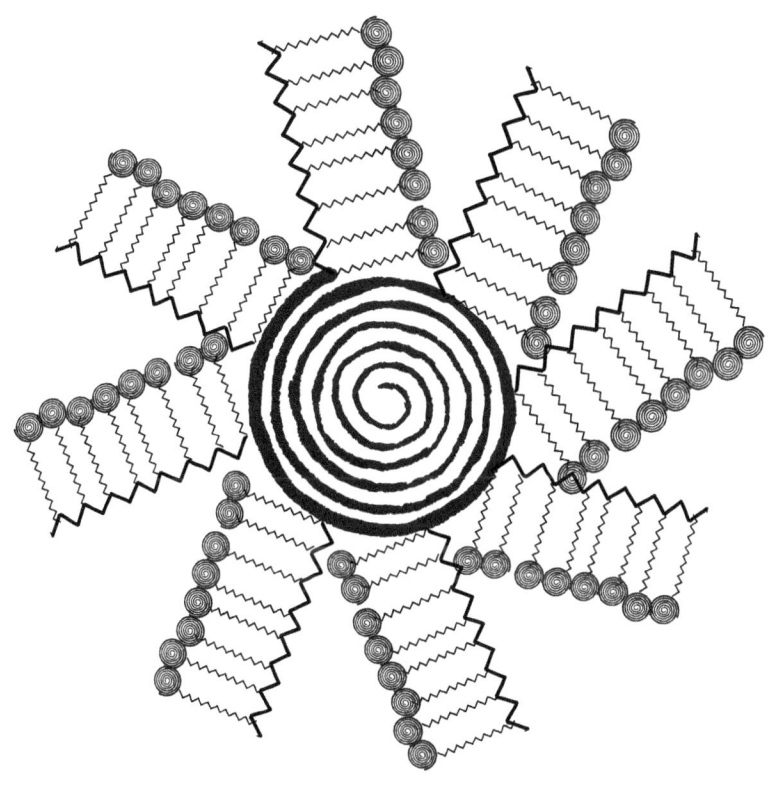

BRAIWAINWAIZWAI
The force that invokes the highest power
of the soul

ZRIKRINRIRRINRIRNRI
The force that restores the water element

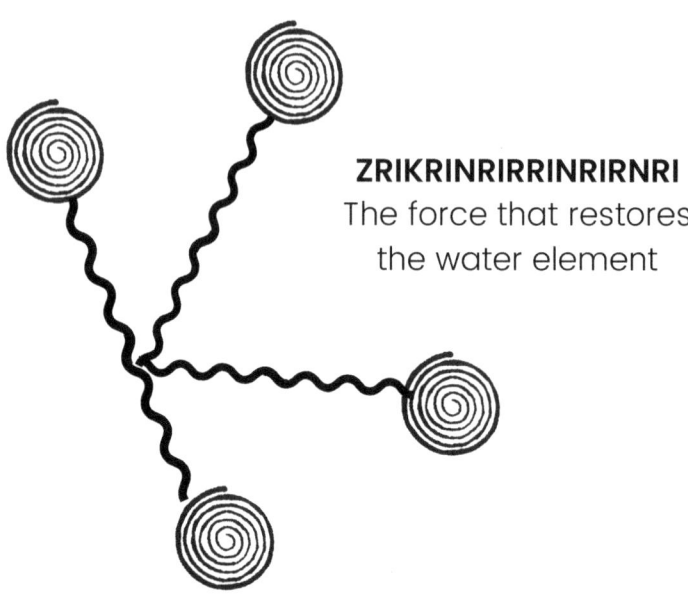

GRAIZWAINWAIKRANKRAI
The force that reconnects the mind, body & soul to the highest force.

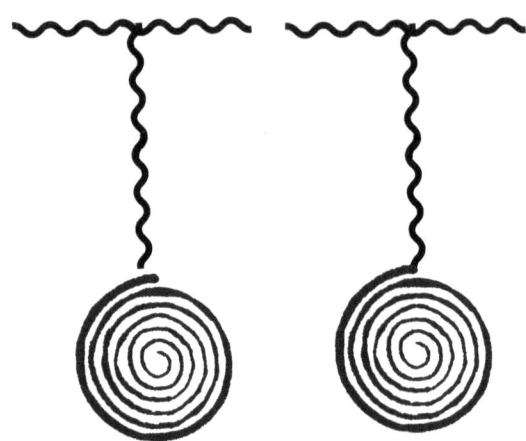

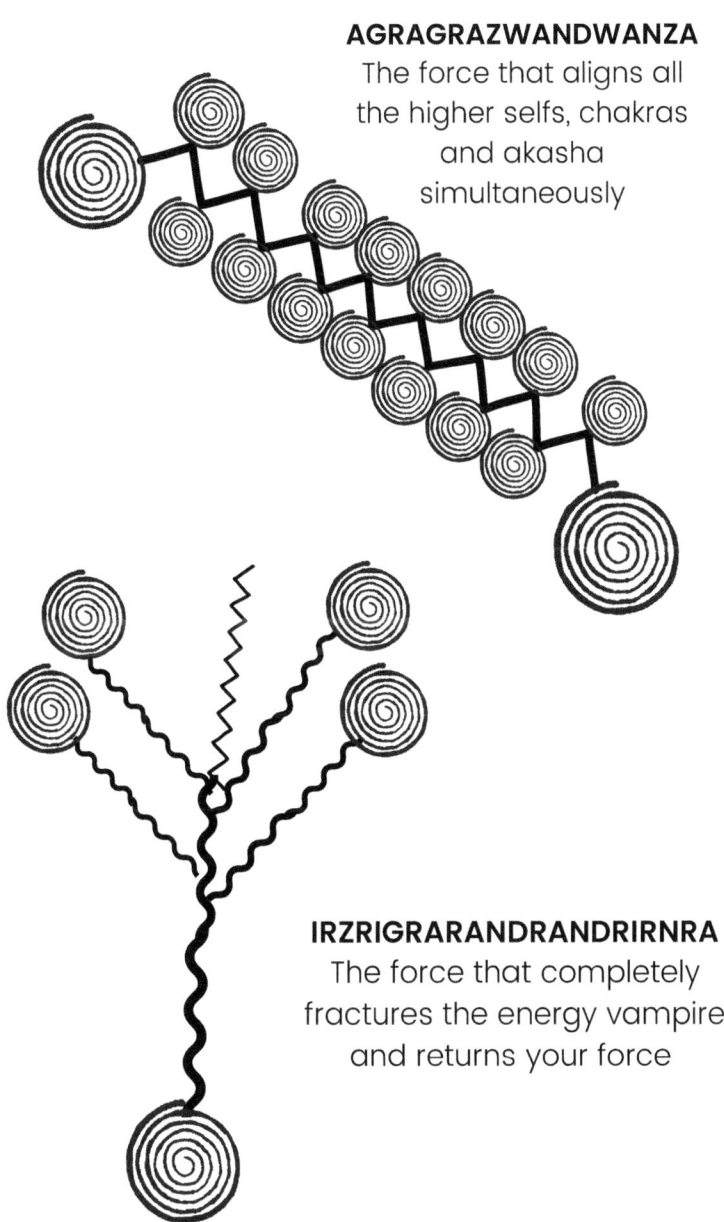

AGRAGRAZWANDWANZA
The force that aligns all the higher selfs, chakras and akasha simultaneously

IRZRIGRARANDRANDRIRNRA
The force that completely fractures the energy vampire and returns your force

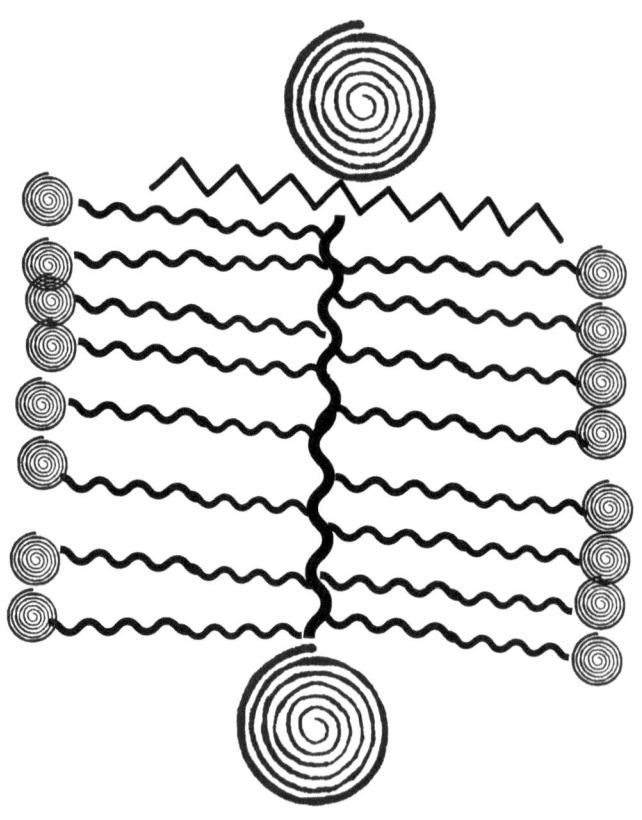

ZAKRAI ZWANKANAZWI
The fire that restores the DNA completely

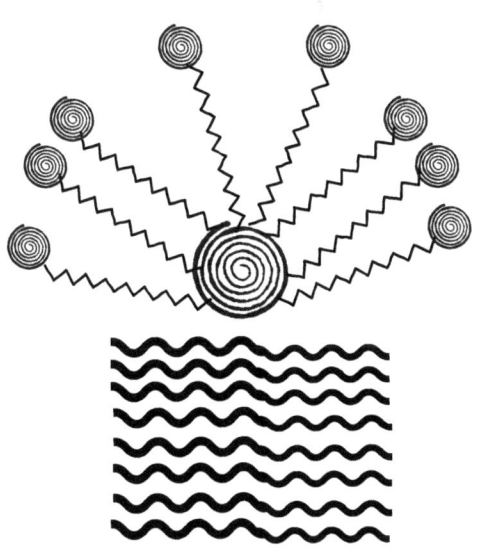

GRAGARANDRANCRA
The force that returns all energy stolen

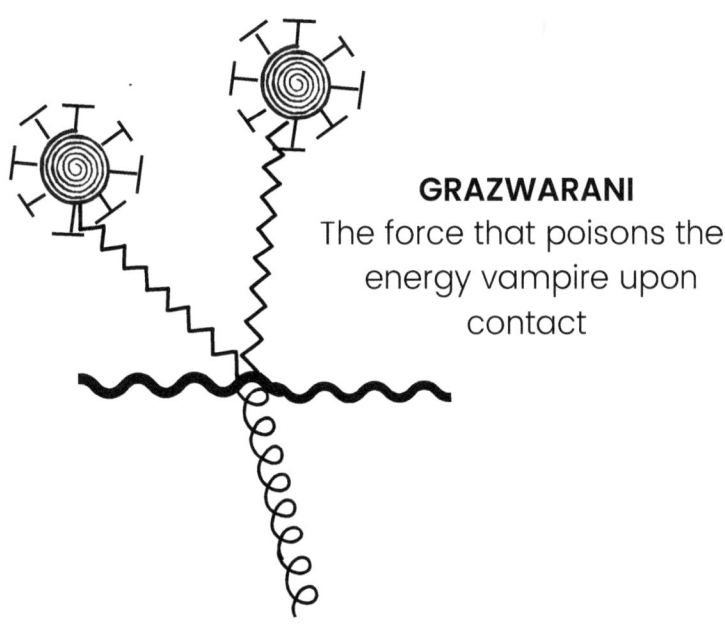

GRAZWARANI
The force that poisons the energy vampire upon contact

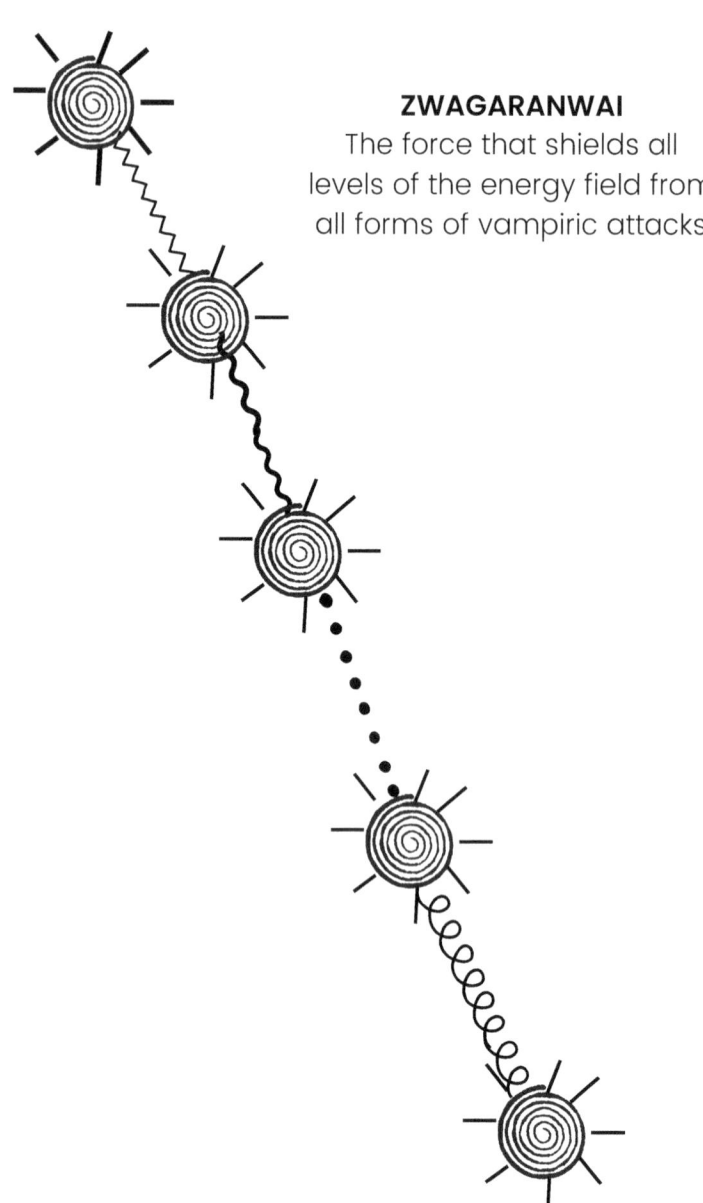

ZWAGARANWAI
The force that shields all levels of the energy field from all forms of vampiric attacks

IWANGWAZAKWANKWATRAN
The force that shields all spiritual products and systems I engage with from delays, overlays, tampering and negative energy

NOTES

www.ingramcontent.com/pod-product-compliance
Lightning Source LLC
Chambersburg PA
CBHW041627220426
43663CB00001B/35